LONGMAN ORIGINALS
Series editor: Rober

GOODBYE Summer Blues

Philip Prowse

Illustrations by Howard Gerrard

Longman

Addison Wesley Longman Limited,
Edinburgh Gate, Harlow,
Essex CM20 2JE, England
and Associated Companies throughout the world.

First Published 1995
Second impression 1996

Set in 11/13pt Melior, Adobe/Linotype (postscript)

Produced by Longman Singapore Publishers Pte Ltd
Printed in Singapore

ISBN 0 582 08143 2

Contents

CHAPTER ONE

The visit

There's one big problem about being a private detective. If you don't work, you don't get paid. I sometimes wonder if I'm in the right job. Then I remember how it all started.

My name's Steven Jackson. My friends call me Steve. I live and work in Los Angeles. I used to be a police officer in this city. I made a lot of friends, but I made one enemy too. I discovered that a few police officers were accepting money from criminals. In other words, they were taking bribes.

That's when I made my big mistake. I told my boss, Sergeant Todd, about the bribes. He just leaned back in his chair and laughed.

"Sure," he said, "everyone takes bribes. I suppose you want your share?"

He opened a drawer in his desk and took out a fat envelope.

"Here, take this," he said. He threw the envelope at me. It was full of money. There must have been at least 5000 dollars in it.

I looked at Sergeant Todd. I did not like what I saw. I felt very, very angry. I thought of all the honest officers I worked with. They didn't deserve a boss like Sergeant Todd. How could I go on working with this man?

I threw the money in his face. I handed in my police badge and I left the police at once. I'm not sorry about that.

That was three years ago. Since then I've been working on my own as a private detective. I like it. At least you never know what's going to happen next.

It was a Monday morning in late July and everything was too quiet. I was sitting in my office with my feet on the desk. There was no mail. The phone wasn't ringing. I didn't have any visitors. I also didn't have any money. I needed money to pay for my car. I'd just bought it. It was a midnight blue Chevrolet. I loved it, but I had to pay 200 dollars a month for it. So I was unhappy. I had the blues – the summer blues.

My office is on the tenth floor of the Belfont Building on Hollywood Boulevard. There's a glass door with my name on it, a small waiting room, a desk, three chairs and a cupboard.

I looked at my watch. Ten o'clock. Time for coffee. I took the elevator to the ground floor, and walked to Al's Diner. I left the office open. You never know. Maybe a millionaire would call to see me.

I was wearing a dark blue suit, a light blue shirt, a smart red tie, blue socks and black shoes. As you've probably guessed, blue's my favourite colour. My eyes are blue too. Blue eyes, curly blond hair – I used to be quite handsome. That was before my nose was broken in a fight on Vermont Avenue. But that's another story.

I finished my coffee at Al's Diner and walked back to the Belfont Building. I took the elevator back up to the tenth floor. I stopped outside my office. There was a shadow beyond the glass door. Someone was in the waiting room. The visitor was holding something – through the glass it looked like a gun.

I waited. The person in my office raised the gun. I kicked the door open. I grabbed the visitor's legs. We both fell over onto the floor.

"Good morning, Mr Jackson," the visitor said. "Do you always welcome visitors like this?"

It was a woman's voice! In her hand the woman held a big cigarette lighter – not a gun! There was an unlit cigarette in her mouth. She stood up quickly and looked down at me.

"I asked if you always welcomed visitors like this. Or don't you like smokers?" she said.

The woman lit her cigarette and blew smoke down at me. She was wearing a smart jacket and trousers. She had short black hair and green eyes. She looked about twenty-five. She also looked a million dollars!

I felt really stupid. "I'm sorry," I said. "I thought you were a man with a gun."

"Get up," the woman said with a smile. "You do look silly lying on the floor. Do I look like a man?"

I sat up. I smiled back at the woman.

"No, you don't look like a man at all," I said. "You look beautiful."

The woman stopped smiling. She kicked my shoulder. I fell backwards.

"Now, listen, Jackson," the woman said angrily. "I've got a job for you. And I don't care what you think about my looks. All right?"

"OK," I replied. I got up and walked over to my desk. My shoulder hurt. I sat down behind my desk. "Won't you sit down?" I asked politely.

"I prefer to stand," the woman said. "About this job I've got for you. How much do you charge?"

"Two hundred and fifty dollars a day, plus expenses," I replied.

"All right," the woman said. "I want you to find someone – a man. If you find him I'll pay you. If you don't, I won't."

I thought for a moment. "OK," I said. "But I'll need 500 dollars in advance." I needed the money for the car. The woman gave me 500 dollars.

"The man's name is Mark Spate," she said. "He works for Metro Rent-A-Car on Los Feliz Boulevard. He's been missing for a week." The woman gave me Mark Spate's photograph and his home address.

"How about your name and address?" I asked.

"Just call me Ann. It's not my full name but it's enough for you," she said.

"And your address?"

"You don't need my address," she answered. "I'll come here, or telephone you, every day at ten o'clock. Goodbye Mr Jackson, and I'm sorry about your shoulder."

Ann smiled and walked out of the office. I watched her leave. She *was* beautiful. The air in the office was full of the smell of a delicate perfume.

I sat at my desk and looked at the photograph. It had been taken by a swimming pool. Mark Spate was wearing red swimming shorts. He was medium height, aged about twenty-five, with quite long brown hair. He had a big nose and an even bigger smile.

I left the office and drove down to Los Feliz Boulevard in the Chevrolet. The Metro Rent-A-Car office was very near Griffith Park. I parked the Chevrolet and went in. A blonde woman in a red suit was standing at the counter. She was tall and slim. She had a badge on her suit saying 'Hi, I'm Suzy'.

"Good morning, sir. How may I help you?" the woman asked.

"I'm looking for a friend of mine called Mark. I believe he works here," I said.

Suzy looked at me strangely for a moment. "You'd better ask Mr Vargas, but he's talking to someone in his office right now," she said.

"I can wait," I replied, and sat down on a chair. A few minutes later a man came out of Vargas's office. He was wearing sunglasses and a leather jacket. He was also wearing cowboy boots. They looked very expensive. Without a word, he walked straight past Suzy and out into the street.

When I went into his office, Vargas was looking out of the window. He was a short, fat man in his fifties. He turned round, and I could see he was sweating a lot. His face looked very red.

"What do you want?" he asked.

"I'm looking for Mark Spate," I replied.

"Never heard of him!"

"He works here," I said.

"I'm the boss. I know who works here, and there's no one here called Mark Spate," Vargas said. His face got even redder.

"I see," I said slowly and walked out of his office.

"Thanks for your help," I said to Suzy. She looked at me but said nothing. I smiled and gave her my card.

"Here's my phone number," I said. "Call me if you remember Mark."

Suzy started to say something. Then she stopped and looked round. Vargas was standing in his office doorway. I waved goodbye and walked out to the Chevrolet.

Ann had given me Mark Spate's home address. Apartment 132, 113 Emerson Avenue, near Wilshire Boulevard. I got into the Chevrolet.

It took me more than half an hour to drive to Emerson Avenue. Apartment 132 was on the first floor. I rang the bell. No reply. I knocked on the door and waited. Nothing happened. I listened. No sounds. I took a plastic credit card out of my wallet. I pushed the card carefully in between the door and the frame next to the lock. The card pushed back the lock and the door opened.

Mark Spate's apartment was quite small. In the living room there was a large expensive stereo and lots of cassettes and compact discs. I switched on the stereo. A cassette started playing. I smiled to myself. The song was an old favourite of mine. It was *Goodbye Summer Blues.*

I searched the apartment quickly and carefully. I was looking for anything that could tell me where exactly in Mexico Spate had gone. There was a row of books on a bookshelf. There were books about swimming. There were maps of Los Angeles. There were several books about Mexico. But there was nothing that told me more than I knew already!

I looked round the room and scratched my head. There were some pictures on the walls. They were photographs of Spate at a swimming competition. There was a label on the back of one of them: "City Swimming Cup. Men's 100 metres free-style. Winner – Mark Spate."

I went into the bedroom. The bed wasn't made. The wardrobe was open. There were jackets and trousers in the wardrobe. I started to search the jackets. I found a small piece of paper in one of the pockets. On the piece of paper it said: "*Casa Dorada*, El Mayor." I shook my head. Where was El Mayor?

At that moment I heard a man's voice behind me. I tried to turn round but the man stopped me. He pressed something hard into my back. It felt like a gun.

"Who are you?" he asked.

I didn't answer. He pushed the gun harder into my back.

"Answer," he said.

I looked up at the mirror in front of me for a moment. I could see only part of the man behind me. He was wearing a leather jacket.

"Who are you?" he demanded again. Suddenly he twisted my arm. I felt a terrible pain. Whoever he was, he was an expert at his job.

"Are you a police officer?" I asked him.

"I'm asking the questions!" he replied. "Not you! Tell me who you are!"

"Let's play a game. You answer my questions and I'll answer yours," I said.

"Oh. You want to play games, do you?" the man said softly.

I looked back in the mirror. This time I could see the gun in the man's hand. It was above my head. I began to turn around but then I felt a terrible pain in my head. I fell to the floor but just before I hit it, I saw a pair of very expensive cowboy boots. It was the last thing I remembered.

CHAPTER TWO
The warning

When I woke up, I was lying in some bushes in a park. I had the feeling that I was still in Hollywood somewhere. Of course, there is a small park on the corner of Vermont Avenue and Hollywood Boulevard. My head felt very heavy and my arm hurt. I looked at my watch. It was 6.30. Had I been unconscious all that time?

I found a public telephone and dialled the number of a cab company. When the cab arrived, I told the driver to take me back to Emerson Avenue.

My blue Chevrolet was still in the parking lot outside Mark Spate's apartment. I walked up the stairs to the apartment. The door was open. I went in. The apartment was a mess. All the books and cassettes were on the floor of the living room. The pictures were broken. In the bedroom all the clothes had been thrown on the bed. Who had searched the apartment? Had they found what they were looking for?

I went out again. The next apartment was number 134. I knocked on the door. After a moment an old lady answered the door.

"Police," I said. "There's been some trouble in number 132. I wonder if you heard anything?"

"Yes," the old lady replied. "I think there was a fight and someone was hurt. An ambulance came."

"Thank you very much," I replied.

An ambulance? That was interesting. Mr Leather Jacket must have some medical friends. A doctor perhaps? My arm was still hurting. I looked at it. I could see a very small mark. Someone had given me an injection. That was why I'd been unconscious for so long.

I left Emerson Avenue and drove to the University

Swimming Pool. It was eight o'clock. I knew someone who worked there. His name was Barney. He was one of the men who cleaned the pool.

When I found him, I took out the photo Ann had given me.

"That's funny. You're the second man today who..." Barney said, but then stopped and looked around.

"There's a coffee shop just outside the main entrance. Meet me there in ten minutes," he whispered.

I went to the coffee shop and waited. When Barney came in, he looked nervous.

"What were you going to tell me, Barney?" I said. I had known Barney back in the days when I was a police officer. He didn't say anything.

"I helped you once, Barney. Don't you remember?"

"Sure I remember, but...," Barney said, and then stopped talking again.

"Well, I need your help now, Barney. Who was the other man who asked you today about Mark?"

"He was a man with sunglasses and..."

"A leather jacket? Is that what you're going to say? And I'm sure he wears expensive cowboy boots, too. Am I right, Barney?"

"How did you know?"

"Have you any idea where Mark Spate is now?" I asked.

Barney shook his head.

"No, but the last time he was here, I heard him say something about Mexico."

"Thanks, Barney. You've helped me a lot," I said, and left.

I needed some sleep. It had been a very busy day and it was getting late, so I drove west along Wilshire Boulevard. I reached Santa Monica and smelled the ocean through the car window. It's a long drive home but I love the beach. My apartment is only a few hundred metres from the ocean.

I got up very early the next morning and looked out of the apartment window. A yellow car was parked across the street. A man was behind the wheel, reading a newspaper. He was wearing sunglasses and a leather jacket. I knew he was wearing expensive cowboy boots, too, even though I couldn't see them.

I had a cold shower and ate a big breakfast. Then I dressed and went outside. The yellow car was still there. The window nearest the driver was open.

"Have you been here long?" I said and laughed.

"Why don't you take a long swim in the Pacific, Jackson," the man said and closed the window.

I got in the Chevrolet and drove towards my office in Hollywood. The yellow car followed me.

"OK," I thought to myself, "let's have some fun, cowboy!"

I decided to drive along Sunset Boulevard. It's wide and has a lot of curves as it goes through Beverly Hills. I overtook a lot of cars. I looked in the mirror. The yellow car was still behind me.

"He's a good driver," I said to myself. Then I looked ahead again. My heart almost stopped.

Two men were crossing the road right in front of me. They were carrying a very big sheet of glass. I put my foot hard on the brakes. Nothing happened!

The men carrying the glass looked at me. They stood still. I could see the fear on their faces. I closed my eyes. I think they closed theirs, too.

With a loud crash the Chevrolet went straight through the glass. I took the car out of gear and slowly brought it to a stop at the side of the road. I looked in the mirror. The two men were still holding the broken ends of the sheet of glass. I got out and slid under my car. Someone had cut the brake pipes.

The yellow car stopped near me. I was still lying under the Chevrolet. The driver got out and walked over. All I could see were his cowboy boots. I pulled myself out from under my car and looked up at his leather jacket and sunglasses.

"Listen, Jackson," he said. "This is a warning. Stop asking questions about Mark Spate." Before I could answer, he got back into the yellow car and drove off.

I stood up. My new trousers were covered in dirt and two angry men were standing by the car. They wanted me to pay for the broken glass. I gave them my card.

It took me more than an hour to get to my office in Hollywood. I had been sitting on a bus thinking about my car. I wasn't feeling very good. The elevator was broken, so I had to walk up the ten flights of stairs to my office. I could see that the waiting room was empty. But as I went into the office I noticed a smell of perfume in the air. Ann was sitting at my desk.

"You're late, Jackson," Ann said. "I told you ten o'clock. I've been waiting for over half an hour."

I sat down on the edge of the desk. I looked at Ann and laughed. Ann's eyes flashed. She looked more beautiful than ever.

"What's so funny?" she asked. "I'm paying you to work, not laugh."

"Not any more," I answered.

"What do you mean?"

"I'm not working for you any more."

She didn't say anything.

"Since I met you yesterday, "I continued, "I've been hit on the head, I've been drugged, and someone has tried to kill me."

Ann looked worried. "What happened?"she asked

I told her what Suzy at Metro Rent-A-Car had said. I told her about Mark Spate's apartment. I told her about the swimming pool and the man in sunglasses. I told her about the Chevrolet's brakes and the crash.

"You gave me 500 dollars," I went on. "I'll have to pay at least 300 dollars for the broken glass. My car's damaged and

I'll have to buy a new pair of trousers. I've had enough. Get someone else to find Mark Spate!"

Ann looked at me for a moment. Then she stood up and put her hand on my arm.

"I'm sorry, Mr Jackson," she said slowly. "I haven't been completely honest with you. There's something I haven't told you."

"I think there's a lot you haven't told me. I don't even know your last name."

She lit a cigarette. This time, when she blew the smoke out, she blew it away from me.

"My last name is Spate," she said slowly. "I'm Mark's sister. I'm from Dallas, Texas."

I looked at her, but I didn't say anything. I wondered why she didn't have a Texas accent. She went on talking.

"I came to visit Mark last week. But Mark wasn't at his apartment. I had a key so I went in and waited for him. He didn't come home. I stayed in the apartment that night. The next day I went to Metro Rent-A-Car. The man there – Mr Vargas – said Mark didn't work there. But Mark called me that evening. He said he was somewhere in Mexico, and that he had gone there to get a car someone had rented from Metro Rent-A-Car."

"In other words, Vargas lied to you when he said Mark didn't work at Metro Rent-A-Car."

"Exactly. Anyway, Mark said he would be back here in Los Angeles the next day. That was last Tuesday. But he never came back. I waited until Thursday. I went back to Metro Rent-A-Car and tried to see Vargas again. I wanted to find out why he had lied to me. I also wanted to know where Mark was and why he hadn't come back."

She stopped. I had a feeling there was something wrong with her story. I didn't know if I could really believe her.

"Go on. What happened when you went back to Metro Rent-A-Car?"

"Vargas refused to see me. So I went to the police. I spoke to a detective. He said lots of people decide to go to Mexico and never come back because they like it there. Then he told me he didn't have time to find out if Mark had ever worked for Metro Rent-A-Car. He said he had too many other cases to deal with that were really important."

'Why didn't you tell me this yesterday?" I asked.

"I was afraid you wouldn't take the case if I did."

"Why?"

"Because I know private detectives like you don't want trouble with the police. That police officer didn't do his duty. It would have been easy for him to find out if Mark had ever worked for Metro Rent-A-Car. But he didn't."

I thought for a moment. "What was the police officer's name?" I asked.

"Todd," Ann said. "Sergeant Todd. Do you know him?"

I didn't answer the question. I stood there, thinking. I still didn't know if I could really believe her story. But I knew I could believe one thing – what she had told me about Todd.

"OK," I said at last. "I've changed my mind. I'm going to help you."

Ann smiled. "What's the next step?" she asked.

"Well, *I'm* going away to Mexico for a few days," I said.

"What do you mean? I thought you were going to look for Mark."

"I am," I answered.

"Then I'm coming with you."

I smiled. "Don't be silly," I said.

"I'm not being silly. If you want to find Mark, you're going to need me, Jackson."

"Why?"

"Because I'm his sister. I know the way he thinks."

"OK, you can come – but on one condition."

"What's the condition?"

" Don't call me Jackson. Call me Steve."

She smiled."Meet me at the Hollywood Roosevelt Hotel. Meet me there in three hours, Steve," she said.

CHAPTER THREE

A trip to Mexico

After Ann had gone, I sat still and thought. Then I remembered something. The Chevrolet! No brakes! I couldn't drive anywhere. And I had to meet Ann in three hours.

I worked quickly. I phoned my garage in Santa Monica and asked them to collect the car and to repair it. Then I phoned for a cab.

I locked the office and walked to the elevator. Good. It was working again. I went down to the ground floor. The cab was already waiting for me.

"Metro Rent-A-Car, Los Feliz Boulevard," I said.

Suzy, the blonde woman in the red suit, was at the desk when I got there. She looked a little nervous when she saw me again, but she smiled when I told her I wanted to rent a car for a few days. She asked for my credit card and gave me a form to fill out. Then she looked quickly round the office. We were alone.

"I'm sorry I couldn't answer all your questions yesterday," she said quietly.

I nodded.

"Mr Vargas told me not to say anything. But Mark *did* work here," she added quickly.

"When did you last see Mark?" I asked.

"Last Saturday – the day Mr Vargas sent him to Mexico. One of our cars was there. Mark had to bring it back here. On Tuesday morning the car was back here but Mark had disappeared," Suzy said.

"Are you sure?" I asked. "Why did Vargas tell me he never worked here?"

Suzy looked nervous again.

" I don't know, but I was in Mr Vargas's office that Monday

morning when his phone rang. I've never seen Mr Vargas look like that before."

"What do you mean?" I asked her.

"I mean I've never seen him look so afraid before. He asked me to leave him alone. So I did. A few minutes later, he called me back into his office. Then he told me that if anybody asked me about Mark, I should say I didn't know him and that nobody called Mark had ever worked here."

"Just one more question, Suzy. You said Mark went to Mexico. But where in Mexico?"

"I... I've already told you too much. I don't want any trouble," she said.

"It wasn't a place called El Mayor, was it?"

Suzy didn't answer my question, but the look on her face told me I was right.

"Thanks, Suzy. You've been very helpful," I said with a smile. "Just don't tell Mr Vargas I was here."

The rented car was a Corvette – a good, fast car. And it was blue! But it took me more than an hour to drive to my apartment in Santa Monica, get some clothes and then drive to Hollywood Boulevard. I was late again!

Ann was waiting outside the Hollywood Roosevelt. She was wearing jeans and a red blouse. She had a small bag with her. I took it from her and put it in the back of the Corvette.

"I'm sorry I'm late," I said.

"Never mind. Where are we going?"

"Mexico," I answered.

"Where in Mexico?"

"You'll find out. Just trust me," I told her.

It was a long, empty road along the coast to the border. Ann was very quiet. As we left Los Angeles, I asked her a few questions.

"Your bag was very heavy. What's in it?"

She looked at me for a few seconds.

"Cameras," she said.

"Cameras?"

"Yes. I'm a photographer."

"Really? What sort of pictures do you take?" I asked

"Weddings, children, families, that sort of thing," she said.

I wanted to ask Ann more, but she leaned back in her seat and closed her eyes. I had a feeling she wasn't really asleep. We drove on, with the blue Pacific on our right and desert on our left. We passed San Diego and crossed the border at Tijuana. An hour later I turned inland and drove on until we arrived in a small town. Ann suddenly opened her eyes.

"Where are we?" she asked.

"El Mayor. Now we have to find the *Casa Dorada*," I said. "I think that means 'Golden House'."

It was late and I was getting hungry again. I saw a small cafe with a supermarket next to it. We went into the cafe and ordered some enchiladas. When the waiter brought them to us, I asked him in Spanish where the *Casa Dorada* was.

"It's at the end of that road," he answered in English, and pointed.

After we finished the enchiladas, I went into the supermarket and bought some food for breakfast. Then we drove for about ten minutes in the darkness until the road came to an end by a lake. The *Casa Dorada* was an old wooden house near the water, and it didn't look very golden. There were some small, white cabins behind it but there weren't any lights on in any of them. I parked in front of a sign that said: *Casa Dorada – Cabins to Rent.*

The entrance hall was empty. There was a desk with a bell on it I rang it. Nothing happened. I rang the bell again. Silence.

Ann pointed to a large book on the desk. It was a register of the names of the people who had stayed at the *Casa Dorada*. We looked through the pages. There were several American names. But no Mark Spate. Then we noticed something. A page had been torn out of the book.

"It's the page for last week – when Mark was here," Ann said.

Suddenly someone spoke behind us.

"Can I help you?"

I turned. A thin, dark-haired man in his late thirties was standing at the door. He didn't smile.

"I'm Hank. I'm the manager." He was an American and spoke English.

"We'd like a cabin for the night," I said.

"I'm sorry. We're full up."

Hank walked quickly to the desk and closed the register with a bang.

"It's getting late," I said. "We need somewhere to stay. Could you please check? Perhaps this will help." I gave Hank ten dollars. He looked at the money and shook his head. I gave him ten dollars more.

"OK," he said. "I've just remembered. There's one empty cabin. It's cabin thirteen and it costs 50 dollars a night. You pay now." He still didn't smile.

Cabin thirteen was very close to the lake. Anne went in first.

"There's a kitchen, bathroom, living room and bedroom," she told me when I brought in the bags and the food from the car.

"All right. You can sleep in the bedroom and I'll sleep in the living room," I said.

"No. I've got a much better idea," Anne answered. "*I* sleep in the cabin and *you* sleep in the car."

She opened the door. I smiled and I walked out. I'm a gentleman. I never argue with women.

The back seat of the Corvette was quite comfortable. I lay back and soon fell asleep.

I woke up suddenly just as the sun was rising. I heard a noise. I looked up and saw a yellow seaplane in the sky.

I had a pair of binoculars in the car. I stood behind the Corvette and watched the plane fly very low over a raft in the middle of the lake. Someone threw something out of the plane. The plane circled and flew away to the west, in the direction of the Pacific Ocean. I looked back at the lake and saw something else. A small red flag was floating on the lake near the raft. I was sure it hadn't been there before. Then I heard another noise. This time it was the engine of a small boat. There was only one person in the boat – Hank – the man who had told us all the cabins were full. He steered the boat past the raft and towards the small red flag. He stopped for a moment and then came back. I was still behind the Corvette with my binoculars. When Hank reached the shore, I could see he had a metal box. It wasn't very large and it didn't look very heavy either. Hank took it into the house.

I went round to the back door of cabin thirteen and knocked. There was no answer, so I turned the handle. The door opened.

I went in. The door to the bedroom was open, too. The bed had been slept in and Ann's bag was on the floor, but she wasn't there.

I thought for a moment. But I was hungry again. I don't think well when I'm hungry. I decided to cook some eggs and make some good, strong coffee.

I was eating when Ann came in through the back door.

"Where have you been?" I asked her, "I was worried,"

"Yes, I can see that," said Ann. "You were worried that I'd come back before you'd eaten breakfast!"

"No, really," I said. "I *was* worried. And I've got something to tell you."

"Let me guess," said Ann. "You saw a plane fly over the lake. Something with a small red flag was dropped. Hank came out in a boat and got it."

I looked at her in surprise.

"I've got photographs of the plane," Ann said, holding up her camera.

"You don't need a detective," I said. "You'd make a good detective yourself."

"Perhaps. And you'd make quite a good cook," she added, looking at my breakfast. "Are you a good swimmer, too?"

I was surprised by her question. "I'm not bad. Why?"

"I want to swim out to that raft. And I don't want Hank to see us. Let's do it now."

A few minutes later we were in the woods. We walked through the trees until we came to the lake. Anne was wearing a plain blue swimsuit. She dived in without a sound and began swimming underwater. I followed her. I swam for as long as I could and then had to come up for air. When I looked around, I saw Ann come up, too. She was far in front of me. She breathed deeply and then went under again. She was swimming like a champion. I wondered where she had learned to do that. She said she was from Texas. Not many swimming champions come from Texas.

When we reached the raft, we saw that it was anchored to the bottom of the lake by a rope. We dived down, following the rope to the bottom. The water was dark. Then Ann pointed at something.

It was a man's body – and it was tied to the rope. There were heavy weights around his feet. I wanted to get a good look at his face but there was no air left in my lungs. I went back to the surface. Ann followed. When we got there we took deep breaths. Then Ann looked at me.

"It's Mark," she whispered. "I know that red shirt."

I hadn't noticed the red shirt. The only thing I had noticed was the terrible pain in my lungs.

"I want to be sure it's him," she said.

We swam down to the body again. I turned the head so that we could see the face. It was a man of about fifty. There was a red hole in his forehead. And it definitely was not Mark Spate.

CHAPTER FOUR

On the *Coromandel*

When we got back to the cabin, we were silent for a few minutes.

"That was Mark's shirt," Ann repeated slowly.

"Where did the man in the lake get the shirt?" I asked.

"I don't know," she answered. "But it means that Mark must have been here."

"If he was, there's a good chance he stayed in this cabin. The other cabins don't look as if they have been used for a long time. Perhaps he left something else here," I suggested.

We searched the whole cabin. Nothing. I sat down on the bed and stared at the floor. It was hopeless.

"We don't even know what we're looking for," I said.

Then I noticed something. A small piece of yellow paper was sticking out from underneath the bed. I pulled it out. It was a printed tourist ticket. On one side it said:

Ensenada Seaplane Tours.

I turned it over. On the other side, someone had written one word – *Coromandel*. I showed the ticket to Ann.

"That's Mark's writing. He must have bought that ticket in Ensenada. Perhaps he's still there," she said.

"There's only one way we can find out. Let's go there."

Ensenada is a town on the coast. When we got there, it was lunch time.

"Let's find out about Ensenada Seaplane Tours," Ann said.

"What do we do then?" I asked her.

"I don't know. Have you any ideas?"

"Yeah," I said. "Let's have lunch. We have to think – and I don't think well when I'm hungry."

We found a small cafe near the beach. After we'd eaten, I called the waiter over and showed him the ticket.

"It's a seaplane that takes people on sightseeing tours. It's down there," he told me, and pointed down the coast.

We drove down to the place where the seaplane tours started. I stayed in the car, while Ann went off for a ride in the plane. After about half an hour, she came back. She looked excited.

"When I was in the plane, we flew over a ship. It's out there, just below the horizon," she said.

"What's so unusual about that?" I asked.

"Just listen! I looked at the ship through the telephoto lens of my camera. I could just see the name on the side – *Coromandel.*"

"There must be a connection between the seaplane and the *Coromandel,*" I said. "Let's watch and see what happens."

We watched the yellow seaplane all afternoon. Each trip lasted fifteen minutes. There were usually four or five passengers. The seaplane always flew around the harbour and then out to sea. Then it came back again. It made twelve trips, and they were all the same.

But the thirteenth trip was different. This time there were two passengers. One was a well-dressed man of about fifty, with white hair. The second was Hank, the manager of the *Casa Dorada*. When I saw him, I told Anne, "Thirteen is our lucky number today!"

The plane took off. This time it didn't go around the harbour but flew straight out to sea. It was flying very low, in the direction of the setting sun. I turned to Ann.

"It must be taking Hank to the *Coromandel*. I want to get closer to the ship. Wait here for me until I –"

"No," Ann interrupted. "*We're* going out there together."

I smiled. I was slowly getting to know Ann.

We rented a small motorboat. Ann took her small camera with her. I started the engine and pointed the boat in the direction of the sun.

The sun went down and it became dark but we could see the lights of a ship ahead of us. Soon we were close enough to see the name of the ship – the *Coromandel*. Ann touched my arm and smiled.

I turned off the engine. Most of the ship was quite dark. There were some lights on the top deck. It was a very warm night but a cool breeze was blowing over the water. The engine of our boat was quiet, and I hoped nobody on the ship could hear us as we came up very close in the water. A ladder was hanging down the side of the ship. I tied the motorboat to the ladder. Then Ann and I climbed up to the ship's lower deck. Everything was quiet and dark. We moved silently round to the other side of the ship.

Ann pointed to some steps and we climbed them. We crawled on our hands and knees towards the lights at the back of the ship. When we reached the end of the deck, we carefully put our heads over the railing and looked down.

We were just above the main deck. It was open at the back of the ship. Five people were sitting around a table. Four were men and one of them was Hank from the *Casa Dorada*. The person next to him was the pilot of the seaplane. He was about forty and had a beard. The third man was wearing a cap and was probably the ship's captain. The fourth was the man with white hair I had seen with Hank earlier. He was talking. A woman sat beside him. She was about thirty, with red hair. The white-haired man had a metal box in front of him.

Ann leaned forward with her camera and took photographs of the people round the table. No one looked up at us. They were all watching the white-haired man. He looked round the table. Then he smiled, opened the box and took out a packet. He gave it to the seaplane pilot, who cut through the paper with a large pair of scissors. The packet contained thousands of dollars! The pilot counted them carefully. Everyone watched in silence as he finished counting and gave the money to the captain.

Then the captain got up and went into a cabin. When he came back, he had another packet. He gave it to the red-haired woman. She opened it and small bright stones poured out onto the table. The woman examined them carefully. She touched them gently. I remembered reading that real diamonds always feel cold. Then she put one finger in her mouth and touched some of the stones with it. They stuck to her finger. False diamonds would fall off easily.

Ann moved closer to the railings to take some more pictures. I reached out to stop her. Just at that moment the seaplane pilot sat back in his chair and looked up. He shouted. He had a gun in his hand. He fired. The bullet hit the railing just above Ann's head. I pulled her back. The pilot fired again. We ran back along the top deck towards the front of the ship and the stairs that we had climbed before.

"There's only one way we can get to the motorboat now. Come on!" Ann shouted. She climbed over the rail and dived into the water.

I was just about to do the same when I looked back and saw the captain. He was running towards me with a knife in his hand. I turned to face him. I jumped back. The captain raised the knife. As it came down, I grabbed his arm and hit him in the stomach at the same time. He made a strange "Aagh..." sound and he dropped the knife. I hit him again. He fell over towards me. I pushed him back as hard as I could. Suddenly the captain was in the air, falling over the rail into the dark water.

I jumped and hit the water near the captain. I swam towards the motorboat. Ann was already in it and reached out with her hand to help me over the side. We turned on the engine and pointed the small boat back towards the shore. There were some shots from the ship but we were already too far away. We kept our heads low. I turned the engine up to full speed.

"I don't think they can see us," I shouted. We raced along in the darkness for five minutes. The lights on the shore were coming closer. I turned round. There was a much larger motorboat behind us. It had a powerful light, but we were too far away to be seen. The boat was going directly towards Ensenada.

Another ten minutes passed. I zig-zagged in different directions but we were getting closer and closer to the shore. At the same time, I could hear the sound of a much louder engine. I looked up, and my heart almost stopped. The seaplane was in the sky above us.

The seaplane flew high above us and then turned. It was flying very low and was coming directly towards us. I saw four or five flashes. Someone was shooting at us from the plane. And this time the bullets were coming from a sub-machine gun. Several of the bullets hit our boat. The engine made a coughing noise and we began to lose speed.

"Jump!" I shouted at Ann.

"What about you?" she shouted back.

"I'll follow you!"

She dived in. I could hear the seaplane coming towards me again, this time from the back. I jumped out of the boat and into the water. Moments later, a shot from the plane hit the fuel tank of the motorboat. There was an explosion. The sky was no longer dark, but red. The plane flew straight into the flames from the boat.

I swam deep into the water and then came up again. Parts of the seaplane were in the water. Oil was burning on the water, and in the light from the flames, I saw something else – the body of the pilot.

I swam away towards the beach. Where was Ann? There was no sign of her. And what about the other motorboat? Where was it? I was getting very close to the beach, and when I put my foot down in the water, I touched the bottom. I walked through the water and stepped onto the beach. A figure came towards me in the darkness. There was salt water in my eyes and I couldn't see very well.

"Ann?" I called quietly.

The figure came nearer. It was Hank.

CHAPTER FIVE
The break-in

I fell to the sand on my knees. Then I raised my head a little and saw a gun in Hank's hand.

"Where's your pretty little partner?" he said angrily.

Hank's gun was so close I could almost smell the oil he used to clean it.

"Where is she?" he said again.

"Are you looking for me, big boy?" a voice said behind him. It was Ann.

As Hank turned around, she brought her hand down sharply on his wrist. He dropped the gun. Then she kicked him in the stomach. It was a karate kick, and Hank fell head down in the sand.

She pulled me to my feet. We began to run. Then I saw the Corvette. It was parked beside the beach, not very far away. Anne jumped into the car beside me and turned the car towards the main highway north.

A shot rang out behind us. Hank must have found his gun in the sand.

"It's time for us to go back to Los Angeles. I don't think we're welcome here any more," I said.

Ann crawled into the back of the car and changed into some dry clothes. Then she drove while I did the same. I was too tired even to think. Ann continued driving, and I fell asleep beside her.

When I woke up again, the sun was just coming up. We were on a freeway south of Los Angeles, and I was hungry again.

We stopped at a McDonald's near the freeway. I got some breakfast for us both. The hot coffee and eggs helped me to start thinking clearly.

"Where did you learn karate?" I asked her. She stared at me.

"I took some classes once," she answered.

"But how...?" I began.

"No more questions this morning. All right?" she said.

I could see she was very tired. We got back in the car and I drove the rest of the way to Hollywood. Ann didn't speak. Neither did I. We went straight to the Roosevelt Hotel.

"If you don't mind," Ann said, "I need some sleep today."

"Yeah. I need some sleep, too. I'll call you later today."

I drove the Corvette to the Metro Rent-A-Car office on Los Feliz Boulevard. It had just opened. Suzy was there.

"Hi," she said when I gave her the keys. "Did you have a good time?"

"Yes, thanks," I replied. "I went to Mexico."

"Mexico?" she said, and looked nervously at the door of the manager's office.

I leaned closer to her.

"Yes. I wanted to find out what Mark Spate was doing there."

Suzy looked worried. I could see she wanted to talk.

"I liked Mark – a lot," she suddenly said.

"What kind of work did he do for you?" I asked.

"He cleaned the cars for us. He often had to take them to the customer. Sometimes he had to drive the car back here."

"Yes, I remember. You told me that's why he went to Mexico. Strange, isn't it?"

"What's strange?" Suzy said. Her eyes looked very big.

"Why should anyone rent a car from you, drive to Mexico and just leave it there?"

"I don't know," she answered, and looked at the door of the manager's office again.

"Please tell me, Suzy," I said gently. "I want to help Mark."

"I really don't know. The clinic has rented lots of cars from us but..."

"Wait a minute, Suzy. Which clinic are you talking about?"

"Dr Summers' clinic. His clinic rents the cars from us. Usually someone from the clinic drives the car to Mexico and then brings a patient back to Los Angeles in it. But last time the driver had an accident and the patient decided not to come. So Mr Vargas sent Mark there to drive the car back here."

" Do you know what happened to the driver?" I asked.

"He had some kind of accident. I don't know more than that."

"Did you see the man from the clinic who drove the car to Mexico?"

Suzy was getting more nervous. She bit her lip several times.

"Was he about fifty years old?" I asked

"Yes," she answered. She looked very surprised.

I described the man I had seen in the lake, but I didn't tell her about the hole in his head.

"Yes, that's what the driver looked like," Suzy said.

Suddenly the manager's office door opened. Vargas was standing there.

"Suzy, for God's sake, what are you doing?" he shouted. Suzy bit her lip.

"Don't you remember what that man, Walter, said? He said he'd kill both of us if we told anyone about these things!" Vargas shouted.

It wasn't necessary to ask who Walter was. I already knew. Walter was the man with the sunglasses, the leather jacket and the cowboy boots.

"He isn't going to kill you, Mr Vargas. Because you aren't going to tell him that you've told me about Mark!" I said.

Just before I left, I asked Suzy one last question.

"Did Mark Spate have a Texas accent?"

"Yes, he did," Suzy told me.

I looked back at her as I walked out. "You did the right thing," I told her.

I took a bus back to Santa Monica and went to my garage to collect the Chevrolet. When I got back to my apartment, I looked up Dr Summers in the telephone book. He had two numbers, one for a house in Beverly Hills and one for his clinic in Hollywood. I drew a line under the address of the clinic. It was on Dundee Avenue, near Griffith Park.

"Tomorrow would be a good time for a visit," I thought. Then I called Ann at the Hollywood Roosevelt Hotel. I wanted to tell her what I had found out and explain my plans for the next day. But she wasn't there, so I left a message.

"Tell her Steve called. I'm going to the Summerview Clinic in Hollywood tomorrow morning. Ask her to be in my office at three o'clock tomorrow afternoon."

I sat there thinking? Who was Ann? Where had she learned karate? If she was really from Texas, why didn't she have a Texas accent? Was she really Mark Spate's sister? If she wasn't, why was she looking for him? I was beginning to like Ann, even though I didn't believe her story. Perhaps I was beginning to like her too much.

The next morning I drove back to Hollywood in my Chevrolet and parked outside the local telephone company. Frank, an old friend from my police days, worked there, and he owed me a favour.

Frank whistled when I told him what I needed.

"Just this once, Steve," he reminded me.

When I left the telephone company, I wasn't in my Chevrolet any more. I was in a small truck that belonged to the telephone company, I drove it to Dundee Avenue.

There was a small hill next to the clinic. From the top of the hill, I could see who came to the clinic and who left it. I could also see the side entrance to the clinic. An ambulance was parked next to it, but it didn't move all morning. I was there for more than three hours and nothing happened. I was beginning to get very bored.

At last, things began to happen. A big white Cadillac drove up to the side entrance and two men got out. One was wearing sunglasses, a leather jacket and cowboy boots – Walter. The other was Sergeant Todd. They disappeared into the clinic. A few minutes later, they came out with another man. He was well-dressed and had white hair. It was the man I had seen on the ship. He *had* to be Dr Summers!

The Cadillac drove off. They were probably going out to lunch. The thought of lunch made me hungry, but there was something I had to do first. I took a uniform from the back of the truck. Like the truck, it had the name of the telephone company on it. I put on the uniform. Then I drove the truck up to the main entrance of the clinic.

A man was sitting at a desk in the entrance hall. He looked up when I came in.

"There's a problem with one of the phones here. I've come to fix it," I said.

"Nobody has told me anything about it," the man said.

"Of course not. It's a technical problem and you won't notice anything at first. But if it isn't fixed, it'll get worse. Call your boss. Tell him it could be serious."

"The boss has just gone to lunch," the man said.

I took out some papers with the name of the telephone company on them.

"Is your boss someone called Summers? Dr Leo Summers?"

"Yes," the man answered.

"And what's his extension?"

"Two-one-nine."

"That's it," I said. "The problem is with his phone. Extension 219. Look!"

I showed the man the papers but took them away before he had a chance to look at them carefully.

"I suppose it will be all right, if I take you to his office," he said slowly.

The office was on the third floor. The man unlocked the door with one of the keys he had on a big ring. We went in but he stood there, watching me. I unscrewed the bottom part of the phone, showed him some wires and said, "Look. That's the problem. One of the wires is badly connected."

I worked on the connection for a moment and then looked at the man again.

"Please go downstairs and call me here."

The man's eyes narrowed.

"Why?"

"Because it's the easiest way to test the phone," I told him.

He thought for a moment and then went out. I could hear him get into the elevator.

I went straight to the big desk in the middle of the room. I had my tools with me and I worked very fast. A minute later all the desk drawers were unlocked.

I put the phone back, and it rang immediately.

"Yes, that's fine. Now, just wait there for a moment while I contact the telephone company. They'll call you in about a minute," I said to the man downstairs,

I looked through all the drawers but found nothing. I knew my time was nearly up. I was angry. I hit the side of the desk with my fist. Suddenly I heard a 'click' and a small drawer opened in the side of the desk. The only thing in that drawer was a thin, black notebook. Inside, I found a list of colours:

Blue
Blue-white
Finest white
White
Silver
Finest light brown

Next to the colours were numbers and dates. Then I saw the word 'carats' and I understood. 'Carats' is the word which describes the quality of diamonds. The colours were different kinds of diamonds and the numbers were the value of the diamonds in carats. I took out my small camera and photographed the list.

It was time to go. I put the notebook back in the secret drawer and closed it. Then I walked back down the corridor to the elevator. I was beginning to feel pleased with myself, when the door of the elevator opened. Three men got out. One was Dr Summers. One was Walter, in his leather jacket and cowboy boots, and the third was Sergeant Todd.

CHAPTER SIX

Patient or prisoner?

I knew where I was, without opening my eyes. I was still in the Summerview Clinic. Someone had tied me down on a hard hospital bed and I could smell the smells of a hospital. I kept my eyes closed. I could hear a man and a woman talking to someone:

"We'll give you one last chance," said the man. I opened one eye for a second. It was Dr Summers. "How did you know there were diamonds in the car?"

There was no reply.

"Where are the diamonds now? Where did you hide them?" Summers continued.

"Give him some more of that truth drug," someone said. It was Sergeant Todd's voice.

"Hasn't he had enough?" the woman said.

"I don't think so. Give him some more," Summers ordered.

There was a pause. Then Summers continued.

"When you left the *Casa Dorada*, the diamonds were in the back of your car. But you weren't supposed to know that. You stopped outside El Mayor, but only for a few minutes. We know because we followed you. And when we stopped you on the other side of El Mayor, the diamonds were no longer in the back of the car. So what did you do with them?"

I suddenly realised who Summers was speaking to. It could only be Mark Spate. And either he couldn't or he wouldn't answer Summers' questions.

Summers' voice grew angry.

"Answer ! Or do you want Walter to get the information from you?" he shouted.

Spate said nothing. Then I heard Summers say something to Todd. The next thing I heard was the sound of a fist, and

Spate gasping with pain.

"No," the woman shouted, "Hitting him won't help. He's full of drugs. "

Summer's voice was cold and hard. "I know what I'm doing. Be quiet!" Then a second later he spoke to Mark Spate again.

"Tell me. Or I'll leave you alone with Sergeant Todd."

When Spate finally spoke, his voice was so low I could hardly hear him: *Casa...Casa Dor...Casa Dorada...*in the w..." The voice stopped.

"You've given him too much of the truth drug. He's fallen asleep again," the woman said.

I heard Summers speak to Todd again. "I'm afraid the nurse is right, Sergeant. There's only one thing we can do now. We'll take him back to El Mayor. Then he can show us where the diamonds are hidden."

"And what about my old friend, Steve Jackson here?" Todd asked.

"You know what to do with him. But don't do it here, not in the clinic. And wait until it's dark," Summers told him.

"Don't worry. It'll look like an accident," Todd answered with a laugh.

"The nurse will prepare Jackson. Now come with me. There's something else I want to show you," Summers said.

I heard the door close. I waited a minute and then opened my eyes. It was late afternoon. The sun was going down. I wondered if I would see it again.

I was only able to move my head a little, but it was enough. I could see that there was another bed in the room. A man of about twenty-five with long brown hair was tied to it. His eyes were closed and he was breathing deeply. It was Mark Spate. So I had found him at last, There were only a few problems. Neither of us could move. We were in the Summerview Clinic. And nobody there was very interested in our health.

I remembered something. When I had searched Spate's apartment on Emerson Avenue, the cassette on the stereo was *Goodbye Summer Blues.* Spate must have left the cassette as a clue. 'Summer' could mean Dr Summers. But what did 'blues' mean? I closed my eyes. I was so tired. It was difficult to think. Spate had said the diamonds were 'in the w...' – what did he mean? And why and how had Summers brought him back to Los Angeles?

I don't know how much time passed before I opened my eyes again, but when I did, it was dark. I was alone in the room. The other patient had gone. Had I dreamed it all? Had I really seen Mark Spate? Or was it the effect of the drugs?

The door opened and Todd came in. He was smiling, and the nurse was with him.

"Awake at last, are you? Good. Well Steve, perhaps you'd like a little exercise now." He laughed again and looked at the nurse. She had a needle in her hand.

She put the needle in my arm. A few seconds later she took it out again. At first I thought I would fall asleep. But instead I could feel my heart beating faster and faster.

"Untie him," Todd said to the nurse. She followed his order.

"Now stand up," he said to me. I tried, but my legs felt very weak, as if they didn't belong to me. My heart was beating even faster and I was sweating. The nurse helped me to stand up. I had to hold on to the bed with one hand.

Todd smiled and hit me hard in the stomach. I fell to the floor and couldn't move. I wanted to vomit but my stomach was empty.

'Don't do that! Not here!" I heard the nurse say.

Todd rolled me over with his foot.

"Did you hear that, Steve? Isn't she a nice nurse? She's really worried about you," he said.

"I don't care what you do to him, as long as you don't do it here. I've given him something which will make him helpless for two hours. Now get him out of here," the nurse said.

They put me in Todd's car. I sat there helplessly.

"Remember. He'll be like this for two hours. That's all," the nurse told Todd before he started the engine.

Todd drove fast. Once we stopped for some traffic lights. I

wanted to kick the door open but I could hardly move my legs. Another car stopped next to us before the light turned green. I wanted to open my mouth to scream, but I could hardly move my lips. Todd turned the car up a road that went high into the Hollywood Hills. Suddenly I knew where he was taking me. There was a road at the top which very few people ever used. It led to a hill that looked down over Hollywood. It was dangerous up there. Not so long ago someone had fallen from the top of the hill to a road far below. Nobody who fell from there could live to talk about it later.

When we got to the top of the hill, Todd stopped the car. He pulled me out of the car. I tried to look around. I had the feeling we were all alone up there. I fell to my knees. Todd dragged me along the grass towards some trees. Then he pulled me to my feet, and suddenly stepped back.

I almost fell again but then I saw where I was. I was standing on the very edge of the hill. Below me there was only a road, and it was a long, long way down. Above me there were the branches of an old tree growing right on the edge of the hill. I grabbed one of the branches with both hands to steady myself. I had just enough strength in my arms to hold on for a few seconds.

Todd laughed again. He was enjoying himself.

"Let's see how long you can hold on to the tree, Stevie boy."

1401

Suddenly I saw the lights of a car. It was coming towards us very fast. Todd looked back. I could feel my hands slipping away. I had to find just a little more strength in my useless arms.

The car came to a stop behind Todd's car and three people jumped out – two men and a woman.

"Drop that gun, Todd," one of the men shouted. He and the other man were pointing automatics at him.

The woman ran straight to me and pulled me back from the edge. It was Ann.

I don't know what happened then. Everything went black.

When I woke up, I thought I was back in the Summerview Clinic again. Then I looked around. The sun was shining through a window. Ann was there. A nurse was there, too, and it wasn't the one I had seen in the clinic.

"I think he'll be all right now," the nurse said to Ann.

"What time is it?" I asked.

"Six o'clock in the morning. How do you feel?"

I moved my arms and then my legs. They were beginning to feel like my own arms and legs again.

"Better, a lot better. But where am I?"

The nurse smiled. "St. John's Hospital, in Santa Monica," she said, and left the room quietly.

For a moment, neither Ann nor I spoke. Then she pointed to some photographs she had with her.

"I have something here that I want to show you. I think you'll find them interesting."

They were the photographs she had taken in Mexico. One showed Hank taking the box from the lake. In another, Dr Summers was giving money to the ship's captain, and in another the young woman was examining the diamonds.

I looked at Ann. "You're a very good photographer," I said. Then I added, "But you aren't a very good liar."

"What do you mean?" Ann asked angrily. "I've just saved your life. And now you're calling me a liar!"

"Yes, a very beautiful liar. Now, I want to ask some questions. And I want answers."

She began to say something and then stopped. "All right," she said quietly.

"First, what's your real name?"

Ann looked staight at me.

"My name is Ann. But isn't Ann Spate. My real name is Ann Rivers. I'm not Mark's sister. That's all I can tell you now."

"How did you know where Todd had taken me?"

"We put an electronic device in his car. When he came out of the clinic with you, we followed you. We didn't want to get too close, but when he took you to that hill, we realised we had to act quickly."

"Where is Todd now?"

"We have him."

"Who do you mean by 'we'?" I asked.

"I can't tell you. Not yet. But now I need some information from you. And I need it quickly. What did you find out in the clinic?"

I told Ann about the notebook. I told her that I had seen Mark at the clinic. I told her that Dr Summers and Walter had taken Mark away. "I'm sure they've gone to the *Casa Dorada* to look for the diamonds," I said.

"I'm going to the *Casa Dorada* too," she said.

"And I'm going with you."

"You can't. You'll need at least another two days of rest," she said.

"We're going there together!" I shouted.

She smiled.

CHAPTER SEVEN

Return to the *Casa Dorada*

When Ann and I left the hospital, there was a car waiting for us. There were two men in it, and they were both wearing dark grey suits. We drove straight to Santa Monica airport. I didn't ask any more questions. I knew I wouldn't get any answers – not yet, anyway.

The car drove through the gate of the airport towards a small jet on the runway. Ann and I got in and the plane took off. I looked out of the window. We were flying south along the coast. I could see waves and beaches. Another man in a dark suit brought us something to eat.

Soon we were over San Diego. I started to think about my visit to the Summerview Clinic, and Dr Summers' black notebook. The song *Goodbye Summer Blues* came back into my head, and I smiled.

"You're very quiet," Ann said. "Are you feeling all right?"

"Yes," I said. "I was just thinking. Blues are a kind of diamond aren't they?"

Ann nodded her head. "That's right – very unusual too."

The plane landed at a small airport near Ensenada. Two men were standing by a car on the runway. One of them was about forty-five and had a neat moustache. The other man was younger.

"Wait here," Ann said and walked over to talk to them. I looked around. There was something strange about the airport. There were no customs officials there. There were no signs that even told me where we were. Ann was still talking to the two men. Then the younger one pointed to another car. Ann looked at me and began walking towards the car. I got in with her and we began driving towards El Mayor.

"Who were those men at the airport?" I asked.

"Please don't ask any questions now. Just trust me," she said.

We got to El Mayor late in the afternoon, and drove towards the lake. We stopped about a kilometre away from the *Casa Dorada* and walked through the woods behind the house and the lake.

My arms and legs still felt weak. I needed a rest already. Ann handed me a pair of binoculars and I looked at the big house. A private ambulance was parked outside. I could just see another car parked behind it.

"The ambulance from the Summerview Clinic is there," I said, "but I can't see anybody outside the house."

Ann had brought a leather bag with her. She took out something that looked like a radio. It was small and black. Then she took out a pair of earphones and plugged them in.

"Did you put an electronic device in the cabin the last time we were here?" I asked.

"Yes. I put in several – in the cabin and in the house."

"But how? And when?"

"You were asleep in your car. Remember? It was still dark. And the *Casa Dorada* is made of wood. These devices go through the outside walls and pick up every sound inside."

She began listening.

"They're in one of the rooms in the house," she told me. Then she gave me another pair of earphones and plugged them into the radio.

I began listening, too. I could hear three voices.

"Do you want me to wake him now?" one of the voices said. It was Hank.

"He's been asleep for almost twenty-four hours. We can use the truth drug again now," another voice said. It was Dr Summers.

"Wake up!" Hank shouted. Then there was another sound. Hank was hitting Spate. I heard a cry of pain.

"Idiot!" Summers said. "I told you to wake him up, not kill him."

"Yeah, but he isn't dead. Look, his eyes are open," Hank said.

"Good. We'll give him another injection of the truth drug now," Summers said. There was silence for several minutes. Then I heard Summers talking to Spate in a low voice.

"The diamonds. Where are the diamonds? Tell me where the diamonds are."

"I told you. They're in the w... in the w...," Spate said in a weak voice. Then he was silent.

"Is he still alive?" I heard a third voice ask. It sounded like Walter, the man with the leather jacket and cowboy boots.

"Yes," Summers said. "But don't hit him. You could kill him. And then we'll never find the diamonds."

"What does he mean when he says 'w...' ? We've checked the walls of the house and every cabin here. We've searched everywhere," Walter said.

"Wait a minute," Hank said. "'In the w...'. Perhaps it means in the *woods*. Perhaps he hid the diamonds in the woods."

There was silence again for a minute or so. Then we saw Summers, Hank and Walter come out of the house. They began walking towards the woods. Ann and I were in the part of the woods closest to the house – and they were coming directly towards us.

"Don't make any sudden movements. Stay as close to the ground as possible," Ann whispered. She began moving towards the lake. I tried to follow her, but I was still very weak. Ann had been right – I did need another two days of rest.

I was much slower than Ann. She reached the water. I saw her head going under. I got up and tried to run, hoping that the three men wouldn't see me through the trees.

Then I heard the sound of two guns firing. Bullets flew through the air just above my head. I looked back. Walter and Hank had reached the woods and could see me clearly. It was hopeless. I raised my arms. It was better to give up now. At least they wouldn't kill me until they were sure about the diamonds. I just hoped I would think of something before then.

Walter reached me first. He pointed his gun at my head. I

sank to my knees. Summers and Hank came up behind Walter.

"What? You're still alive?" he shouted.

"Let me kill him now," Hank said.

"No, you idiot!" Summers shouted at him. "He knows things that we want to know. How did he get here? Is he alone? What's happened to Todd?"

Then he turned to me with a nasty smile. "And you won't get away this time, I can promise you that!"

Just then Walter pointed to the lake.

"Look. There's someone in the water!"

He fired his gun wildly into the lake. Ann dived under the water again.

Summers gave orders quickly. "Hank. Take Jackson back to the house. Walter and I are going to catch his friend." He and Walter ran towards the motorboat.

Hank dragged me back to the house and then into a small room. When we got there, I saw Spate lying on a bed. His eyes were closed, but his lips were moving. Hank threw me to the floor and then locked the door. I looked around the room. There was one small window above the bed, but it had iron bars across it. I tried the door. It was thick and strong. I couldn't break that down.

I sat down on the floor and waited. At last Spate opened one eye. "Who are you?" he asked. His voice was weak but I could understand him.

"Steve Jackson, private detective," I replied. "I was hired to find you. Now I've found you. My job is done. The only problem is, we're locked in here."

"Well, my job isn't finished," said Spate slowly.

"Perhaps not, my friend. But it looks like you and I are finished – unless we can get out of here somehow."

"There isn't much time. Listen," Spate said, and began talking.

"I work for the United States Customs. We were sure that Summers was smuggling diamonds from Mexico into the United States. We believed he smuggled the diamonds in cars he rents from Metro Rent-A-Car, but we needed proof. I

got a job at Metro so that I could check all the cars that Summers used."

"You came here because something happened to the driver of one of the cars, didn't you?" I asked

"Yes. They said he had an accident."

I told him about the man at the bottom of the lake.

"How did you find him?" Mark asked.

"I didn't. Ann did. She's a very good swimmer, just like you." I said.

He stared at me.

'Who's Ann?" he asked.

I tried not to show how surprised I was. If he didn't know her... well, that would have to wait.

"Have you any idea why they killed the man in the lake?" I asked.

"He was working for Summers as a driver, but he tried to pass information to the Los Angeles police. Hank found out about it and killed him."

"But how did Hank find out?"

Spate answered with one word, "Todd."

"Did Todd tell them about you, too?" I asked.

"No. Todd didn't know that we were watching him."

"What happened when you came here?"

"I spent some time in Ensenada on Sunday, to see what I could find out. I talked to a mechanic who works at Ensenada Seaplane Tours. He told me that one of the planes often made an early morning trip out to sea and then to El Mayor."

"That's true. I saw it drop a box in the lake," I said.

"I guessed that was how they got the diamonds into Mexico – from a ship. I heard the name 'Coromandel' but I didn't see any ships. When I got here it was late, so I asked Hank if I could stay for the night before I took the car back. He said I could. That night, while Hank was asleep, I examined the car. I knew the best places to look, but I was lucky, too. I found the diamonds. I took them out of the car and hid them here."

"Why did you do that?" I asked.

"U.S. Customs had an agreement with the Mexican government on this one. If we found evidence here in Mexico, we would leave it here. My plan was to hide the evidence, drive the car back to Los Angeles, then tell my people and the Mexican police where the diamonds were. The agreement with the Mexican government was that they would arrest the members of the gang on the Mexican side of the border and we would arrest the people in the United States."

"What happened then?" I asked.

Mark shook his head. "I thought I would call my office in Los Angeles when I crossed the border, to let them know what was happening. But I didn't know that Walter and another man were waiting for me just on the American side of the border. I parked the car next to a public telephone. Before I could dial the number, Walter was behind me with a gun. The other man examined the car. When he discovered that the compartment was empty, they took me to the clinic. You know the rest of the story."

"Not all of it," I said. Mark's voice was getting weaker, but there were still some things I needed to know. "I still don't know where you hid the diamonds."

"I'm a good swimmer. They're in the w... the water," he whispered.

"In the water? You mean, in the lake?" I said.

"Yes. I put them in a place where Summers would never look for them."

CHAPTER EIGHT
Goodbye summer blues

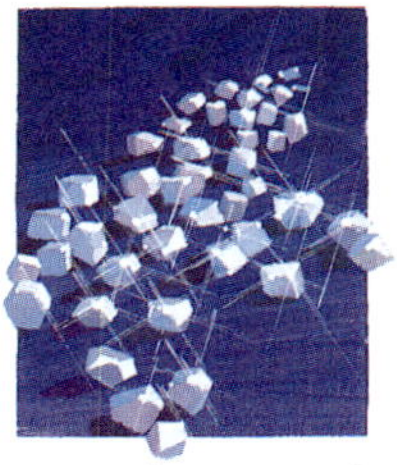

It was very dark. Mark and I had talked for a long time. I had told him all I knew about Summers. Mark had told me exactly where the diamonds were. He was asleep.

I climbed up to the small window and look through the iron bars. I could see some lights in the woods. I was sure that Summers and his men were still looking for the diamonds. I smiled to myself. They didn't know the diamonds were in the lake.

I must have slept for a while, but I suddenly heard sounds inside the house. A key turned in the lock, and the door opened. I looked up. Ann was standing there.

"Ann," I shouted. "Are you all right?"

Instead of an answer, I heard a man's laugh. Summers was behind her. He had a gun in his hand.

"So the diamonds are in the water, are they?" he said.

I stared at him. Had he been at the other side of the door, listening? No, Mark's voice had been so weak that even I had found it difficult to understand him.

"How..." I began to ask. Then I saw a strange look on Ann's face.

"How did I hear your conversation? Is that your question? Ask your friend here!" Summers said. Then he pushed Ann into the room and locked the door again behind her. Spate was still in a deep sleep.

"I'm sorry, Steve. I'm sorry," Ann said. Then she told me the rest of her story.

"After they forced me out of the water, I thought they were going to kill me. But they wanted to know what we had been doing there. They looked around in the woods and Walter found the listening device, where I'd hidden it."

"And then what happened?" I asked. But I already knew the answer.

"Walter knows as much about those listening devices as I do. He and Summers listened to you and Mark. They heard everything."

I looked at her. Could I believe her? I still didn't know who she was. I had mentioned her name to Spate, but he didn't seem to know her. Who was she working for, then?

"What's wrong? Why are you so silent?" she asked me.

I didn't answer.

It was getting lighter now. The door opened again. Walter and Hank were there.

"Get up. We've got a job for you," Hank shouted at Ann. Then he looked at me.

"You, too," he said and pulled me to my feet. Spate opened his eyes again but he seemed to be only half-conscious.

They marched us downstairs and outside the house. Hank and Ann were in front. Walter and I were behind them. Summers was standing on the shore of the lake. Hank dragged Ann over to him. Summers said something to Ann. She shook her head. The doctor spoke again, he looked angry now. Ann shook her head again. Suddenly Summers looked at Walter and pointed to me. Walter pushed me forward. He began to twist my arm behind my back. It hurt terribly. I screamed.

"First I'll break both his arms. And then I'll break his legs," Walter shouted.

"Stop!" Ann cried, "I'll get the diamonds for you."

Ann got into the boat. Hank steered it into the middle of the lake. We watched as the boat stopped by the raft in the middle of the lake. Ann dived in. We waited.

Walter twisted my arm again. "Let's hope your friends are telling the truth, Jackson, or you'll be down in that lake for a long time," he laughed.

At last Ann came up to the surface again. She had a metal box in her hands.

Summers walked over to us. He looked pleased. "It was a good idea, if I say so myself. The box was tied to the weights on the dead man's feet. But of course you already know that. Spate told you," Summers said smoothly.

The boat came back to the shore.

"Give me the box," Summers ordered. He opened it and smiled.

"My diamonds," he said. "Thank you very much."

He turned to me. "You see, there is a perfect system here. So I can't allow anyone to destroy it."

Time was running out very fast. I had to think of something that would make Summers want to talk.

"Yes, a really perfect system," I agreed. "The diamonds are flown from the ship. They're dropped in the lake. Then they're smuggled over the border in rented cars. Is that right?" I asked.

"That's right," Summers said.

"You don't use your own Cadillac because it would be too noticeable. Even the driver of the rented car doesn't know what he's taking across the border. Everybody else thinks the cars are used to bring patients to your clinic."

Dr Summers smiled. "You're very clever, Mr Jackson. Perhaps you should work for me. Unfortunately, I don't think you'll be alive much longer." He nodded to Walter and Hank "Take Jackson and the girl for a walk in the woods. We don't need them now. We've got the diamonds," he said.

"But you've forgotten one thing, haven't you?" I shouted. "We've got Todd!"

Summers' face darkened. " Don't try to fool me, Jackson. I got a message late last night. Todd's dead."

What did he mean? I looked across at Ann. Didn't she say 'We have him?'

Ann said nothing, but she shook her head very slightly. Her eyes warned me not to say anything more about Todd.

"Just one more question, doctor," I said quietly. "Why do you do it? You don't need the money. Why are you smuggling diamonds?

"You're about to die," Summers said. "So'll tell you anyway. I love diamonds. They're the most beautiful things in the world."

The doctor stared up at the sky. There was a strange look in his eyes. "Diamonds are pure. They're innocent. Not like people. People are dirt." He stopped for a second. Then he looked at me again. "I'll do anything for diamonds. They're my life. One day I'll have the finest collection of diamonds in the world," he said.

Somehow I didn't believe him.

"What good are all your diamonds going to do you if you keep them all for yourself and don't sell any of them?" I asked.

"Oh, but I do," he said with a laugh. "It's very simple. I keep only the most beautiful ones. I sell the others."

"Who do you sell them to, doctor?"

"People who make a lot of money illegally, so they can't keep much of it in the bank – you would call them gangsters. They come to the *Casa Dorada* to buy diamonds. They pay for the diamonds here and then I have more money to buy even more diamonds!"

"I don't believe you. I think you're mad!" I told him.

Summers stared at me coldly.

"Kill them," he said to Walter.

Walter and Hank marched us away from the lake and towards the trees. We stopped. I felt Walter's gun in my back. Hank pushed Ann in front of me.

"We'll kill her first. You can watch," Walter whispered into my ear.

I closed my eyes. There were two shots. I waited, thinking I was going to die. Nothing happened.

I opened my eyes again. Someone was lying on the ground but it wasn't Ann. It was Hank. He was dead. And I couldn't feel Walter's gun in my back any more. I turned round. Ann was all right. Walter was standing with his hands in the air. He had dropped his gun. Three men stepped out of the woods. Two were wearing police uniforms. They both had guns.

"Mr Jackson?" the third man asked. He had a neat moustache. It was the man I had seen at the airport. "My name's Jimenez, Captain Jimenez of the Mexican police. I'm pleased to meet you."

"Not as pleased as I am to see you," I replied. "But how did you know we were here?"

Captain Jimenez turned to Ann. "This young lady is wearing an electronic device in the heel of her shoe. We have been following every movement. And now we have definite proof that Summers is not only a smuggler but also a murderer."

I looked at Ann. She smiled.

"You're full of surprises," I said.

We went back to the *Casa Dorada.* Two other policemen were with Summers. For the first time he looked very worried.

"Look in this box. Millions of dollars worth of diamonds are here. Why don't you take them and go? You can share them with your men. You'll never have to work again."

Captain Jimenez didn't even look at the diamonds.

"No, señor. You can't bribe me. I am not like your Sergeant Todd."

The doctor stared at Jimenez. Suddenly his eyes looked dead – as dead as the diamonds he loved. Two police officers took him away.

Mark Spate was brought out of the house and put in an ambulance. When he saw Ann, he smiled.

"Is that who you were talking about?" he asked me. "Her name isn't Ann. It's Jean."

I turned to Ann – or should I call her Jean? She smiled.

"I'm sorry, Steve," she said. "I haven't been completely honest with you. Mark and I were a special team working for the U.S. Customs Service. We couldn't go to the ordinary police when he disappeared. So I asked you to find him. Don't be angry with me."

"Angry?" I shouted. "Why should I be angry? I've been hit on the head, drugged and nearly killed. My new car's been smashed, and I've got no money! And I'm never sure if you're telling the truth!"

"I know I haven't been completely honest..." she began.

I started to laugh.

"But I'm telling the truth now," she went on. "I think you're wonderful."

She walked up and kissed me.

That's the nice thing about being a private detective. You never know what's going to happen next. We walked to the lake. It was still summer. But the summer blues had gone!

READING ACTIVITIES

Before reading

1 *Goodbye Summer Blues* is a detective story. Look at the front and back cover. Where does the story take place? With another person make a list of famous detectives from films and TV from that country.

2 Think about detective stories you have read or seen. What kind of things happen in detective stories? What kind of characters usually appear? Work with another person and compare your ideas.

3 Look at the chapter titles on the Contents page. What do you think might happen in each chapter? Two of the chapters have unusual titles: what do you think *Coromandel* and *Casa Dorada* are?

While reading

1 In Chapter 1, who said

"Sure, everyone takes bribes."
"Do you always welcome visitors like this?"
"Two hundred and fifty dollars a day, plus expenses."
"Oh, you want to play games, do you?"

2 Make true sentences by joining the beginnings in A with the endings in B. The answers are all in Chapter 2.

A
Steve had a small mark on his arm because someone
Steve's car crashed because someone
The woman said that she
Vargas lied when he said Mark
Steve and Ann decided to

B
go to Mexico together.
didn't work at Metro Rent-A-Car.
was Mark Spate's sister.
had given him an injection.
had cut the brake pipes.

3 In Chapter 3, Steve and Ann found a body in the lake at the *Casa Dorada*, but they didn't report this to the police. Can you suggest three possible reasons for this?

4 What did Steve and Ann see on the *Coromandel*? Look at the information on pages 28-29. Now write out the conversation between the people who were sitting round the table.

5 In Chapter 5, who knew that Steve was going to the Summerview Clinic? What do you think will happen next?

6 Go over what you have found out about Sergeant Todd so far. What adjectives would you choose to describe him? What do you think might happen to him in the end?

7 What is the correct order of these events is Chapter 7?

Mark told Steve he had hidden the diamonds in the water. ☐

Hank and Walter caught Steve in the woods. ☐

Ann and Steve listened to what was happening with an electronic device. ☐

Mark told Steve he worked for U.S. Customs. ☐

Summers, Hank and Walter were trying to make Mark talk. ☐

8 Mark told Steve that he didn't know anyone called Ann. Who do you think Ann is? Discuss your ideas with other people in your group.

After reading

1 Imagine the conversation between Steve and Ann as they walked by the lake at the end of Chapter 8. Begin like this:

Steve : Why didn't you tell me who you were...?
And what about my money...?

2 Mark Spate has to write a short report to U.S. Customs about how Dr Summers smuggled the diamonds. Write Mark's report.

3 There is a lot of publicity about Dr Summers' arrest. A newspaper reporter interviews Suzy. Write the interview.

4 A few weeks later, Steve finds this note in his office.

> *Mark Spate said I could trust you. It's about my father. Some secret papers of his are missing and I think he is in danger. Please help me. Call me at home as soon as possible. The number is 436721 – Lisa.*

Will this be a new case for Steve? Make a list of questions for Steve to ask.